A

PERSONAL ACCOUNT OF

THE HISTORY
OF
STEAM

AND

THE
EAST FIFE
FISHING FLEET

BY

PETER SMITH
OF
CELLARDYKE

ISBN 0-9525621-1-1

Photograph on front cover: Drifters landing herring at Anstruther
(From the Cowie Collection courtesey of Bill Flett)

THE HISTORY

of

STEAM

and

THE EAST FIFE FISHING FLEET

by

PETER SMITH
of
CELLARDYKE

Published by:
James Corstorphine
45 Hawthorn Street
Leven, Fife KY8 4QE

Printed in Scotland by Levenmouth Printers

ISBN 0-9525621-1-1

Hauling herring nets on board the Steam Drifter *Pride o' Fife*. The man standing closest to the camera is Salter Watson. The catch must have been a good one as the Engineer and Fireman (at the rear of the photograph) have been called up from the engine room to assist

Contents

The steam drifter *Olive Leaf* berthed at the Middle Pier in Anster. The ropes supporting the propeller indicate that the packing around her propeller shaft, made from lignum vitae wood, was in the process of being replaced. The drifter berthed on the outside is the *Unity*

FOREWORD

<u>"Semper tibi pendeat hamus"</u>. So read the coat of arms of the Burgh of Kilrenny before 1928 when the Burghs of Kilrenny and the two Ansters (Anstruthers) were united. Literally it meant "May the hook always hang in your favour", but the fishers of Nether Kilrenny, vis. Cellardyke, friendly translated it as "ye're aye better wi' a heuk in the water"; and so they fished from time immemorial until Jockie Muir retired in 1984.

It is not possible to find any details about local fishing practice beyond the First Statistical Survey, except perhaps in Gourlay's book *Memorials of Cellardyke* in 1879. Here he mentions on page 28 how a fisherman named Brown was drowned whilst fishing alone with creels in a small boat for crabs or partans to be used as bait for the great lines. This would have occurred in the latter part of the 17th century, as the same man had a son drowned in a disaster in 1800. Each member of a larger boat's crew had to fish for bait in rotation, outside the herring season, the herring being the first choice as bait for cod or ling.

In the first statistical account, 1791-99, the Rev. William Beat writes for the Parish of Kilrenny, stating that there were *"about 10 or 12 large boats in the harbour swimming to the brim with cod, besides 30,40 or 50 strung upon a rope towing from the stern"*. The Rev Jas. Forrester, writing for Anster Wester, mentions *"cod, ling, turbet, hollybut* (halibut presumably), *skate, haddock, herring, flounders caught here and sent to Cupar, Edinburgh, Stirling and Glasgow"*.

This great line fishing was prosecuted in large boats of between 40 and 50 feet, gradually increasing in size to about 60 feet. This remained the largest size of boat until the steam capstan enabled bigger sails to be hoisted than was possible with man power alone. we come to the age of steam when, in the late 1800s, Stephen

Williamson offered the fishermen of Cellardyke the opportunity of shares in a steam trawler. He favoured the trawl but the Cellardyke fishermen opted for steam liners with the exception of one man named Doig who went to Aberdeen in Williamson's trawler. I remember him coming on an occasional holiday, as he used to talk to my great Aunt (who was born in 1854), if she happened to be in the garden when he was passing. She herself was a Doig.

Having introduced the Cellardyke fishermen, their boats and their adventurous spirit which cost many lives, I will close with thanks to John Doig and Jim Tarvit for developing the photographs; to the Scottish Fisheries Museum who, together with Mr T. Boyter, Mrs M. Tarvit, Mr John Horsburgh, Mr Alex Anderson, Mr Robert Gardner, Mr John Dunn, Mr A. Corstorphine and Mr Bill Flett, supplied most of the photographs. Thanks also to Mr John Muir, Mr James Corstorphine, Mr Donald MacDonald and, finally, to Dr. David Malcolm without whose enthusiasm this little book would not have been possible.

Footnote: Throughout this book I shall refer to Anstruther as 'Anster', as this has long been the local pronunciation of the town's name.

Steam Drifters (left to right) *Pilot Star, Spes Melior* and *Calliopsis* berthed at the Middle Pier in Anstruther

The herring fleet wait to enter Anstruther Harbour
c.1930's

Steam and the East Fife Fishing Fleet

The last time I looked up *Who's Who*, the name of the present
Lord Forres was given as Anthony Stephen Grant Williamson,
domiciled in Australia. Either his grandfather or great grandfather
was Stephen Williamson, born at 27 James Street, Cellardyke.
His birthplace has since been pulled down and the garage of a
bungalow is now in its place. The family were efficient businessmen and founded, with Balfour of Leven, the shipping firm of
Balfour and Williamson, who traded between Liverpool and the
Pacific. He was Liberal M.P. for the St.Andrews Burghs from 1880
until 1885, when he lost by one vote after a recount. His benefac-
tions to the town included Chalmers Church and the Waid Tower
and, with Fowler, had the present Cellardyke Town Hall built. He
also paid off the debts of Anstruther Harbour and was the stimulus
which triggered off the coming of steam fishing boats to East Fife
with a letter which appeared in the *East Fife Record* in May 1890.
The letter suggested buying some steam trawlers for East Fife
which he would sponsor in view of the prosperity they had brought
to Aberdeen.

There then followed an article about steam powered fishing in
Aberdeen which said that in February 1882, a few Aberdeen merchants had purchased a small steam vessel from Dublin called the
Toiler which brought ashore, in her first year, catches worth
£2,600. The merchants then equipped some steam tugs for the
trawl which proved a costly failure.

Also in Aberdeen, a steam trawler was constructed, built by John
Duthie & Sons & Co. and called the *North Star*. She first went to
sea in September 1883 and her first year's catch realised £2,635.
Her return in 1889 was £3,710 and, in that same year, 81 trawl
vessels including 73 steam trawlers landed fish at Aberdeen, where
the fishing was now worth a quarter of a million pounds annually.
Letters appeared in the *East Fife Record* for and against

Williamson's proposal, with the chief supporter being M. Doig (Pratt) of James Street, Cellardyke. He was then chosen by Stephen Williamson to be skipper of his new steam trawler, which was built at Kinghorn by G. Scott & Company. Williamson guaranteed to buy all surplus shares that were not taken up locally. The new trawler was 105' long by 20'6" by 11' 1" and named the *Faith*. From the letters in the *East Fife Record* it was obvious that the local fishermen preferred the great lines to the trawl. In Cellardyke the great lines were known as the 'gartlins' and in St. Monans as the 'gertlans'.

A gartlins is made up of a 'taes' of line. If you look up 'tae' in the Scottish National Dictionary, it says: *"A section of a deep sea fishing line of varying length having a specified number of hooks, generally 100 or 120"*.

Until the year 1939 in the East Neuk a taes of line was 75 fathoms long, the length of the 'Roperee' shed in Anster belonging to Miss Mitchell's grandfather, the latter lady having taught in Cellardyke school long enough to have included my father as well as myself, as pupils. Before the railways came to Anster, this shed extended from where there is at present a ceramics factory across from the Waid Academy, north-westwards for 150 yards. Later it ran parallel to the railway in the field to the south of the line, much shorter then, and the rope had to be looped to allow for the required length. The late Les. Brown worked there when he left the school and he told me about it. A gartlin was then made up of 6 taes, each containing 120 hooks about three and a half fathoms apart, measured by a man extending his arms horizontally; a fathom being regarded from finger tip to finger tip so that a man with long arms and a broad chest might have fewer hooks per great line than an average man.

Each gartlin was then contained in basket work known locally as a 'scull'.

According to the late Jimmy Brunton, Cellardyke boats of his day

The steam drifter *Pursuit* in St. Monans Harbour

Steam drifters in the Outer Harbour in Anster during the height of the herring fishing industry

The Steam Drifter *Fife Ness* A522 (Later KY27). Her skipper W. Sutherland, nicknamed 'Scow', was also coxwain of the sailing lifeboat *James and Mary Walker*. He retired when the first motor lifeboat arrived and was decorated on his retiral by the Duke of Montrose at a ceremony on the Middle Pier.

went to the lines with 7 men having 5 sculls each and required 8 or 9 boxes of herring for a baiting.

John Muir, who was the last East Fife skipper to go to the gartlins, retired in April 1984. He said that they fished with fewer hooks to a taes and with much rougher rope material. Jimmy Brunton's lines were made of the best Italian hemp from Gourock rope works.

The sailing boats of the East Neuk pursued this hazardous means of fishing when they were not fishing for herring. They went to the Winter Herring Fishing, which lasted from January until the end of March. The gartlins were worked by the sailing boats from April to June. At the end of June they departed to the north for the Summer Drave, which lasted until the end of August. The boats then went south for 6 to 8 weeks to Yarmouth or Lowestoft, so the gartlins occupied a period of only 2 or 3 months in the year for the sailing boats.

One of the most adventurous of the Cellardyke gartlins men was David Watson (Pip) in his boat *Providence*; only about 60 feet long and, as my fathers brother Dave sailed with him, I heard many stories about him. He was there in May 1895, when W. Motion (Grandfather of retired banker W. Motion), was lost at sea and also in 1896 when A. Tawse was lost.

For all the storms Pip Davie went through, he died while taking a country walk and his body was brought home in a corn cart. He had no family and was the uncle of the late Provost Carstairs.

The Cellardyke fishermen were so renowned for their adventures at the gartlins that the Rev. James Barr, a West of Scotland M.P., on asking one of my father's cousins where he came from was told "Cellardyke", of which he had probably never heard. The Rev. Barr replied that he had indeed heard of Cellardyke, being home to the most intrepid great line fishers on the East coast of Britain.

The Steam Liners - The Companies and the Capital: 1890-1900

If I appear to have dwelt too much on the Cellardyke fishermen and ignored Pittenweem and St.Monans, it is partly because I am a Dyker and partly because Stephen Williamson was prepared to back any company who would build steam vessels either for the trawl or the lines.

On 11th April 1890, Provost Anderson of Anster called a meeting to discuss Stephen Williamson's proposal. There were 30 present and they decided to form a committee made up of W.S.Bonthron, W.H.Anderson, D. Murray, J.Marr, J.Leslie, W.Jarvis (boat builder), D.Cook (lawyer), J.Birrell and J. Pratt; the latter two being fishermen. Together they proposed to invest £1,690. It amuses me to read any subsequent letters from Stephen Williamson as he worked through the lawyer, whom he addressed as Dear Cook (no Mr.). Most of the rest were businessmen.

At their second meeting all thoughts of the trawl were given up and they decided to ask for estimates from a number of builders for a boat 80' long and drawing 9' of water with a 30 H.P. engine to go to the lines.

A sub-committee was formed of Leslie, Cook, Marr and Bonthron. A letter appeared from Capt. John Keay of Liverpool recommending that the new vessels be constructed from steel. Capt. Keay was arguably one of the top 3 masters of the China Clippers.

Estimates came from Anster, Pittenweem, Leith, Eyemouth and Dysart, ranging from £1,950 to £2,375 and, for a steel boat, £3,275. Jarvis of Anster was given the order for a wooden boat costing £2,140, and the Anster Steam Fishing Co. Ltd. was formed. Jarvis built the first steam liner for £2,260 of which Stephen Williamson contributed £500 and, at 2.45 p.m. on the 3rd of October 1891, the steam liner *Maggie Lauder*, KY449, was launched and christened by Miss Jessie Bonthron. The crowd was

Launch of the steam liner *Tulip* from Fulton's yard in Pittenweem

The steam drifter *Pilot Star* unloading her catch at the extreme end of Anster East Pier. In the background, Skipper D.Smith is at the steam capstan and on the pier are A.Smith, J.Carstairs and D.Parker. Note the company name of J.Bonthron & Sons on the fish boxes.

so large it even filled the Potty Pier. All the local shops closed for the launch and pilot Parker fired two rockets. She had an 82' keel and measured 89' overall by 18', drawing 9'6". Her sleeping accommodation consisted of 7 bunks forward and 2 aft for the engineer and fireman and she was towed to Leith for her engines to be fitted by Messrs. Hawthorn. She was also fitted with a steam winch and a patent windlass for the anchor. Her sails were made by sail maker Johnstone, whose loft was located to the east of the dentist's surgery at the front of Whale Close. The first skipper of the *Maggie Lauder* was D. Birrell. I can just remember him, a tall man who lived in the last house at the East end of West Forth Street. She managed her first trip in December, catching 12 score of cod which was valued at £24.13/-. Although it would not have been noticed at the time, something significant had happened regarding the future of the local fishing fleet.

The lady who christened the *Maggie Lauder*, Miss Jessie Bonthron, would be either the sister or aunt of W. S. Bonthron, who had returned to Anstruther after taking a law education, to help run his father's business of J. Bonthron & Sons, fish buyers. The company name of J. Bonthron and Sons was to be seen on fish boxes as long as herring were landed at Anster. He became a well known general auctioneer in the district and ran the business of fish salesmen with his son in law and other partners from the office in the building immediately to the east of the Masonic Arms public house. Bonthron had shares in many of the local fishing boats. £10 shares for a second liner soon amassed £2000 and the keel was laid by Jarvis. The changes included a glass box over the steering gear in front of the funnel. Unfortunately no photograph of the *Maggie Lauder* has been found and the photograph which is in the Scottish Fisheries Museum of the second steam liner was taken years later, when her top hamper had been modernised. Meanwhile, Fulton at Pittenweem had received two orders from North Shields and had laid a keel lengthways in the region of the present Sale Ring at Pittenweem. On 26th April 1892, Jarvis launched his second liner. Christened by Miss Cook, *Rob the Ranter*, KY458, was 88' long by 18' by 9'6" with a 33 H.P. engine fitted at Leith from where she returned in two and a half hours. Her first shot in May, with skipper J. Hodge, was 56 score of which 3 and a half were ling, 22 skate, 11 halibut, realising £43.11.3d. The company then proposed a dividend of 9% and a third liner was ordered at a cost of £2,530.

At the meeting proposing the dividend, a breakdown of the *Maggie Lauder*'s figures were given for her first six months:

Coals cost £133.3.5d.
Engineer and Fireman £80.2.10d.
7 Fishermen £428.8.9d.
Salesman's commission £70.16.4d.
Credit £353.11.11d.

The steam drifter *Camellia* and 'Fifie' sailing boats in St. Monans harbour. The 'Fifie' lying on the outside is KY221 *Sincerity* and lying inside her is KY658 *Fyalls*. *Fyalls* later had an engine installed and was renamed *Brighter Dawn*

Steam drifter KY304 *Kilmany*

The crew of the steam drifter *Anster Fair* KY461. She was built as a steam liner and launched in August 1892. The Author's father, Peter Smith the fisherman poet of Cellardyke, is third from the right leaning on the capstan

Conflict with the Herring Drave

Something unexpected to the landsman bankers now happened. The skippers and crews of the steam liners decided to lay their boats up while they went to the drave in their sailing boats. June 25th 1892 saw the line fishing suspended for three months, although *Maggie Lauder* had her largest shot of 113 score, valued at £75, on June 4th.

The sailing boats, not exceeding 60 feet in length at that time had a crew of 7. The earnings were divided into eight and a half shares, of which the skipper, being the owner, got two and a half shares. Many Highlanders came for the drave, as well as miners from Buckhaven and, having no gear of their own, they were known as Halfdealsmen. This meant that if the skipper put in an extra two fleets of nets and carried two Halfdealsmen, he was earning three and a half shares out of the total of eight and a half shares. It is not difficult to understand that the top skippers were just not available for the summer season. e.g. I have opened my notes at 1888, Sept. 14th. King of the Fishers, David Watson (Pip) of the *Providence* earned £350 of which he might get £140.

The owners and shareholders were now up in arms and it was amusing to see them giving their opinions, drapers to the fore along with one of the local farmers. It was resolved that skippers in future would be engaged for the whole year and this meant that they didn't necessarily get the top men.

The Liner Building Boom - A Chronology

Before the third liner was built, one of the Cellardyke skippers,
John Birrell, bought a boat from Leith named the *Edith*, KY460.
There are no statistics available, but she was small.

1892

25th July: Fulton at Pittenweem launched his steam liner *Teal
Duck*, measuring 86' by 18' by 10'6". She was laid on her port side
and launched down three ways, the tide being so high that the
spectators standing on the Middle Pier got their feet wet with the
wave set up by the launching vessel.

24th August: Anster Steam Fishing Co. launched its third steam
liner. Miss Oliphant christened her *Anster Fair*, KY461. She had
an 88' keel, measuring 93' overall by 19' by 9'8",with berths for the
men all aft. After the engines were put aboard at Leith, a comfort-
able wheel house was fitted. For the second successive time the
bottle did not break at the launch.

On the same day at St. Monans, J. Miller launched a steam liner for
North Shields measuring 84' by 18' by 8'6" named *Hibernia*. There
were now six steam liners working from Anster, the two on hire
being *Fulmar* and *Puffin*. Miller launched another liner for North
Shields measuring 91' by 18'6" by 8' named *Glenavon*.

12th June: The fourth liner for Anster was launched by Jarvis
measuring 96' by 18' by 10' named the *William Tennant*, KY472.
She was christened by Miss Lumsden of Pittenweem and the first
skipper was A. Gourlay. Her maiden trip on February 20th earned
£50. 10. 6d. The profit for the Anster Company's four liners was
£812.16. 7d. on which they declared an interim dividend of two
and a half per cent.

On the week ending 5th May, 1893, 67 sailing boats and 5 liners
filled the East Pier with fish for auction several times for which the
buyers paid out over £1,500.

The *William Tennant*, the fourth steam liner built in Anster. Note that she has no small boat, no casing and no galley. Her sails and jib are ready - showing a lack of confidence in the steam engine!

Rob the Ranter, the second of the steam liners. There is no picture surviving of the first steam liner *Maggie Lauder*. This is obviously not an early picture of *Rob the Ranter* as she does not look as primitive as the *William Tennent*

17th May: Fulton at Pittenweem launched his second steam liner for North Shields named *Shell Drake*, 91 ft. overall.

17th June: The liners were laid up again and new skippers were appointed under contract for a full year. Liners were also to tow 3 boats at 1 shilling per mile up to a distance of 30 miles.

Something funny happened on board *Rob the Ranter* on a voyage from Newhaven to Anster, which normally took two and a half hours. The skipper and the engineer fell out over the dumping of the ashes and the engineer refused to start the engines. In light winds and with all sails set, she took seventeen hours for the trip. The engineer decided to use the engines for entering the harbour in case the boat went ashore and he would get the blame.

7th December: *Glenogil*, KY493, was launched by Jarvis for a new company, the East Neuk Steam Fishing Company. The sum of £2,000 had been raised to form the new company by twelve gentlemen, who included S. Williamson, M.P. W. S. Bonthron was appointed manager. The *Glenogil* was their first vessel, measuring 96' by 18' by 10' and was christened by Miss Marjory Oliphant (daughter of a banker). This time the ribbon broke and the bottle was broken over her bow after she had been towed into the inner harbour for the ceremony. Her first skipper was R. Stewart.

Before the year ended another steam liner, the *Effort*, came from Granton on loan to Cellardyke.

Miller launched a liner named the *Margaret* for Aberdeen, and insurance had been raised per boat to £24.5/- because of the loss of three Aberdeen trawlers.

1894

No new steam liners were launched in East Fife, but Adam Reid, on April 3rd, had a new sailing boat the *Reliance* built by Jarvis. She was 60'9" by 19'6" by 9'8" and what was important was that she had the first steam capstan in the local fleet of sailing boats. This started a new and last rush to build the typical Fifie, which was to last so long in St. Monans. They were now able to build sailing boats up to 70 feet. Before the steam capstan, manpower was only strong enough to hoist sails big enough to move boats of less than 60'. Now the steam capstan was able to hoist a bigger sail, hence bigger boats.

September 7th saw more than the 100 local boats returning from the North with King of the Fishers Adam Reid grossing over £400 in his new boat. There was so little news I see I have a note about one of the steam liner's committee men. The draper Mr. Marr's shop was to be lighted with the new incandescent light.

1895

Anster Steam Fishing Company declared a dividend of 6% and a local skipper, David Parker, brought a steam liner *Bernicia* on loan from North Shields.
Another liner was brought on loan to Cellardyke from Granton named *Roslin*. She was built of steel and skippered by John Mackay.
Two new companies were formed locally. St. Adrian Fishing Company Ltd for Pittenweem and the Forth Steam Fishing Company was founded by S. Williamson and on 27th February, Jarvis launched a new steam liner for them. She was christened by Miss Jarvis and named after Stephen Williamson's house in Cheshire, the *Copley*, KY536. She had an 88' keel, measuring 96' overall by 18' by 10', machinery by Hawthorn of Leith. Her first skipper was D. Wood. Also in February, the *St. Adrian*, KY544, was launched at Pittenweem. Her dimensions were 95' by 19' by 9', with berths for

Launch of the steam liner *St Adrian* from Fulton's yard in Pittenweem

Steam drifter KY218 *Pride o' Fife*

Hauling drift nets on board the steam drifter *Pride o' Fife*

9 men. Her engine, by Hawthorn of Leith, was compound inverted direct acting, surface condensing, and had 21" stroke cylinders. The first skipper of the *St. Adrian* was James Hughes (Ireland).

Her trial trip caused a commotion, and ensued much controversy with letters to the *Scotsman* and the local paper when she went aground on Inchkeith Island. With the tide ebbing, she keeled over, causing some panic. The small boat was lowered and ferried the women and children in relays to a tug which landed them at Leith. Summing it up, it would appear that Fulton, the builder, had asked if he could be allowed to take the helm, and therefore had to make good the repairs. It caused some amusement in the neighbouring towns.

Crail now got in on the act and in May the Crail Steam Fishing Co. was registered. The committee included Provost Peattie of Crail, Mr. & Mrs. Cairns of Ashburn House, Dr. and Mrs. Dow and, as usual, W.S. Bonthron.

22nd August: Jarvis launched the *East Neuk*. She had a 90' keel and measured 96' overall by 19'2" by 10'9", with berths for 9. First skipper was J. Watson (English Jock).
At 3 p.m. the daggers were knocked out and she was christened by Mrs.Cairns, before a large audience of Crailers, the gentry having driven along in horse drawn brakes. The daggers I'm told are the last steel clamps joining the cradle upon which the vessel rests on to the greased fixed runways on the launching slip.

This year saw the first steam capstan installed in a sailing boat in St. Monans. She was the *John & Agnes*, owned by Jock Cameron. She had a safety valve below 122 1b. pressure. It was installed by Beccles and had to be blown down every week and refilled with fresh water.

This year also saw a new ice store built in East Green, Anster, to the east of the Gas Works, where Harbourlea retirement home is now situated. The walls were 21" thick, then a space of one and a half feet to a wooden wall. The space was filled with fine gas cinders, and they had a gas engine to crush the ice imported from Norway. I certainly remember the ice house, but it was only a store in my time.

1896

24th Jan: The Castle Steam Fishing Company was registered, with a capital of £3,500. Messrs. Marr & Williamson wanted the new Castle liner to be built of steel and it was built at Leith by Hawthorn.

In the same week a Danish schooner delivered 250 tons of ice to the new ice store.

Another new company was formed. Notice the local gentry must have thought they were on to something big. Among the shareholders were Lawson of Armfield, Major Sprott of Stravithie, Capt. Scott Davidson of Cairnie, Baillie Darsie etc. and the manager was, of course, W. S. Bonthron.

Another company tried to register as the White Star Fishing Company, but the shipping company of the same name objected, so they registered as the White Cross Fishing Company. The district was dealt a blow by the death of Cormack, who had come to the East Neuk from Eyemouth in 1829. He had become the main fish buyer in the district, having his property at the extreme east end of Cellardyke.

28th April: The first steel liner for the Castle Co. was launched at Leith. She had a 90' keel and her other dimensions were 19' by

The steam drifters *Plough* and *Copious* berthed stem-on to Anster East Pier

The *County of Fife*, the third steel liner built for the Castle Steam Fishing Company

10'6". She was christened *Kellie Castle,* KY567, by Miss Janet Gardner, daughter of skipper P.Gardner. The engine had a compound condenser, pressure 120 lb.

13th May: Jarvis launched the *White Cross*, KY571, measuring 88'8" overall by 18'6" by 9'3". She was christened by Miss A.Thomson of Wellpark before being towed to Leith by a tug named *Earl of Windsor*. She had shelves for 150 score and a thwartship bunker to carry more coal as well as accommodation aft for 9 men. Her first skipper was D.Parker.

14th May: Another steel liner having the same dimensions as *Kellie Castle* was launched at Leith and christened *Isle of May*, KY569, by Mrs Leslie of St Ayles. Her skipper was Dods Watson.

25th August: The third steel liner for the Castle Company was launched at Leith. She was named *County of Fife*, KY572, skippered by Andrew Henderson. On the 25th September she broke the record for a week's work with £179.
The Crail Steam Fishing Co. paid a dividend of 8%.
The steam liner *East Neuk* earned £2,190 from sales. Towage amounted to £108, expenses £1,831, fishermen £702, coals £300, engineer and fireman £183, bait, ice and railway carriage £335. Commissions and dues were £153.
It should be noted that when herring weren't available for bait they often had to send as far as Grimsby for inkfish (squid) as a substitute.

Another three companies were formed before the end of the year. The Kilrenny Steam Fishing Co. was oversubscribed and the manager was W. S. Bonthron. On the 4th November the Bay Steam Fishing Co. was formed, mainly by fishermen John & Henry Bett, R. Hughes, A.Lothian, D. Wilson and P. Murray. They raised

£6,000 for two boats.

17th November: The Ness Steam Fishing Co. ordered the construction of a steel boat named *Fife Ness*.

27th November: Provost Anderson of Anstruther talked to Provost Christie of Pittenweem on the newly introduced telephone. John Marr, chairman of most of the companies, said that he "looked forward to the day when the boats would 'phone in their catches. Science", he said, "had made marvellous advances. What with lady cyclists, motor cars and one could only wonder and say, what next?"

5th December: The skippers of the liners met to discuss their grievances. David Wood (Birrell) was in the chair. He said they should ask for 40/- the baiting, with the wages of engineers and firemen to be paid by the owners. Philip Gardner proposed 50/-, as their working was more costly than the Shields liners, (a baiting was 35 lines). They were bargained up to June 1897 and they wanted a new bargain made before then.

1897
5th February: Jarvis launched the liner *Kilrenny*, KY594, christened by Miss Leslie of St. Ayles. She measured 96' overall by 19' by 10'4" and her first skipper was W. Watson.

12th February: The Anster Steam Fishing Co. held its Annual General Meeting. The amount of fish sales for the year was £9,166, net profit £1,336.7.1d. for 5 liners.

15th February: A new liner was launched at Aberdeen for the Ness Fishing Co., Anster, christened *Fife Ness*, KY 586, by Miss Doig, daughter of Skipper Doig of the *Faith*. She was built of steel by

The Cellardyke steam drifter *Unity* pictured shortly after arriving in Yarmouth in October, 1910

The steam liner *Newark Castle*, the only liner built in St Monans

Hall Russell & Co.; her dimensions being 102' by 19'6" by 10'3", weighing 130 gross tons. She was fitted with compound surface condensing engines of 320 BHP and she was equipped for the trawl. Skipper Adam Reid.

20th March: The liners were laid up as their crews went on strike. This was as a result of the outcome of the skippers meeting held on 5th Dec. when they asked for 40/- for baiting from the owners. Their claims were refused and after some bargaining they compromised on 25/- per baiting plus surplus bait and paying the wages of the engineer and fireman all the year round.

22nd March: Miss May Brander of Johnston Lodge launched the *Largo Bay*, KY598, at Dundee for the Bay Fishing Co. She was made of steel and measured 95' by 18'6" by 10'6", weighing 123 tons. Skipper R. Hughes.

9th April: Miller, building at St. Monans, launched for the St. Monans Steam Fishing Co. Ltd, a steel liner *Newark Castle*, KY661. She was christened by Miss Niven, daughter of Provost Niven, the chairman of the Company and headmaster of the St. Monans school. She was 100ft. long drawing 196" of water. She was towed to North Shields where she was equipped with double expansion engines by Messrs. Tweedie. Her skipper was James Innes (Scott).

14th June: In a downpour of rain, Mr. Jarvis gave the order "down daggers" and Miss McLaren of Inner Gellie House launched the steam liner *Innergellie*, KY604. Her dimensions were 96' by 19'1" by 10'4" and was to be skippered by John Birrell (Tarvit).

30th. July: The local paper reports 'poor fishing by liners', but M. Gardner in the sailing boat *Vanguard* had 104 crans at Aberdeen.

King of the Fishers in his own boat *Lavinia* was D. Birrell who made £540. (He was skipper of the first liner *Maggie Lauder*).

29th. September: Jarvis launched for the Bay Co. the last liner built for local owners, the *Rothesay Bay*, KY611. Measuring 96' by 19' by 10'6", she was christened by Miss Young, Rodger Street, Anster. This liner was later sold to Aberdeen as A885, to be brought back to Anster as KY97, the number I knew her by. I was only to know three liners including *Rothesay Bay*, the other two being the *White Cross* and the *Glenogil*. The *White Cross* was worked as a drifter by A. Gourlay of Cellardyke and his sons up to the 1920's, likewise the *Rothesay Bay* with J.Stewart of Cellardyke as skipper. The *Glenogil* lay at the head of the Anster West Pier for many years before being sold to Granton as a trawler. It was believed locally she was just used as a poacher as she could often be seen on a Saturday or Sunday night sheltering behind the May Island.

In 1897 there also appeared from Dundee the *Curlew*, DE91, built as a trawler but, being unable to get a crew in Dundee, she joined the local fleet as a liner, skippered by T. Watson with a Cellardyke crew.

Seated on the left is Alex Gourlay, skipper of one of the original steel liners. Along with his sons, Alex Gourlay worked the *White Cross* as a drifter until the 1920's. Seated on the right is the author's Uncle, Dave Smith. Dave fished with 'Pip' Davie in the sailing boat *Providence* and was also a crew member of the steam drifter *Olive Leaf*

Gourlay's drifter *White Cross* was built as a liner in 1896 by Jarvis of Anster for the White Cross Steam Fishing Company

The *Rothesay Bay* was the last steam liner built for local owners in 1897. As a herring drifter, she was skippered by J.Stewart of Cellardyke until the 1920's

Steam Drifters (from outside) *Spes Melior, Cassiopeia* and *Lasher* at the end of the East Pier at Anster. The crews are preparing the nets for another trip.

The End of The Line

Shipbuilding still went on in Anster although no more steam liners were to be built.

1897

Eighteen steam liners were engaged from Anster, some on loan, but the crews were becoming dissatisfied. Skippers were giving up after their 12 month contracts were finished, e.g. Skipper Henderson left the *County of Fife* and bought a sailing boat, the *Livelihood*, from St. Monans. There was a general move towards the bigger sailing boats because of the steam capstan, and less worry about expenses and having to land at home ports to please the owners, when better prices could be got elsewhere.

1898

List of Company Dividends.

Anster Steam Fishing Company	2%
Bay Steam Fishing Company	3%
Crail Steam Fishing Company	8%
Castle Steam Fishing Company	3.5%
County Steam Fishing Company	6%
East of Fife Steam Fishing Co.	5%
Forth Fife Steam Fishing Co.	2.5%
Kilrenny Steam Fishing Co.	5%
White Cross Steam Fishing Co.	10%

11th April: Jarvis launched a sailing boat for George Anderson, the *Integrity*, measuring 65' by 20' by 9'6".

2nd September: Jarvis launched the *Maggies*, measuring 66' x 20'6" x 10'3" for Philip, Alex and J. Gardner.

The liners this year fished mainly from other ports as the skippers sought better margins and on April 8th the *Isle of May* had a record landing of £188 from 125 score at Hartlepool.

1899
Compare the prices at the beginning of the year with today. Cod as high as £5.6/- a score, plaice 39/- per 7 stone box, lemon sole 54/- a box, haddocks 16/6 a box.

3rd February saw the start of the breakdown of the fleet. The *Copley* was sold to Shields for £1,950. On February 17th, *Glenogil* was sold to Dundee for £1,900. On February 24th, *East Neuk* was sold to Aberdeen for £2,600.

Stephen Williamson and J. Marr resigned from being directors of Anster Steam Fishing Co. (the first one). The liners were sold off although they kept the company going until 1892.

19th. May: Miller launched the sailing boat *Celtic*, measuring 69' by 21'6" for J. Mackay and the pattern was now obvious, the steam capstan meant bigger sail boats. I have note saying that the bush rope and the steam capstan meant that the drift nets could be worked in bad weather. Notice that in the first years of the steam liners they laid them ashore for three months during the summer while the crews went to the herring drave in their sailing boats. I couldn't understand why they didn't go to the drave in the liners. Before the steam capstan there was no messenger rope below the

Three steam drifters can be seen in the background of this view of St Monans harbour. They are waiting, with steam up, for the high tide to allow them to leave for the East Anglian herring fishing

The St Monans steam drifter *Faithlie* leaving Anster harbour in 1935. Among the drifters in the harbour are *Spes Aurea, North Esk, Norman Wilson* and *Mace*. In the foreground is the Leith registered *Gratitude*

The steam drifter KY228 *Norman Wilson* entering Yarmouth

nets and they still retained the thick rope on the top beside the corks, as they hauled by hand and thus had the assistance of the 'iron man', a system of vertical wheels which was only operated by manpower. I never saw this used, but they could be seen in the 1920's on board the old boats laid up facing the 'Folly' in Anster. So, round about 1899, the messenger came in and the sailing boat's steam capstan pulled in the fleet of nets. That still doesn't explain why the steam liners didn't operate this system.

I asked my friend the late James Brunton of Cellardyke about this, as his father and relatives had bought *Rob the Ranter* in partnership with a local businessman J. Morris, who owned the baker's shop in Shore Street, Anster.

He told me it was because the big propellers tore the nets. They had found a large propeller on Bonthron's premises (Bonthron had become the main fish salesman in the East Neuk by this time and owned the fish premises near East Anster Kirk), and *Rob the Ranter* was stamped on it. This meant that they must have fitted this propeller on to go to the gartlins. She only went a little faster, but when they came to shoot their bait nets to catch their own bait, they tore their nets while shooting them and realised that this was why the original crews had sent away so often for bait.

22nd. September: Jarvis decided to retire and sold his business to Miller of St.Monans, but before that, on 26th July, he launched a trawler for Davidson, fish salesmen in Aberdeen named *Cruden Bay*. She had a 94' keel and was 103' long overall by 20' by 11'6". This was the largest boat to be built in Anster until the M.F.Vs (Motor Fishing Vessels) were built during the last war measuring 115-120ft.

1900

2nd February: Miller's first launch in Anster. A trawler named *Lucania* measuring 100' by 20'6" for Irvine, North Shields.

9th February: Fulton was building bauldies for Fisherrow and expected to get more orders.

23rd. February: A big storm in the North Sea caused much havoc. Locally the Shields liner *Bernicia*, manned by a Cellardyke crew, was lost with all hands, leaving 6 widows and 30 orphan children. The crew was T. Watson (Skipper), D. Henderson, A. Boyter, A. Gardner, A. Murray, J. Stevenson and T. Ritchie. The two black squad men came from Shields.

The success of the herring fishing now made crews desert the liners and the first liners were mentioned as going to Yarmouth fishing for herring, the *White Cross, Rothesay Bay, Glenogil* and *Innergellie*.

A list of the liners is now given and how they were disposed of.

1899

Feb. 3rd	*Copley* to Shields for	£1,950
Feb. 17th	*Glenogil* to Dundee for	£1,900
Feb. 24th	*East Neuk* to Aberdeen for	£2,400

1900

Feb. 23rd	*Bernicia* lost.	
Nov. 9th	*Kilrenny* to Aberdeen for	£2,500
Dec. 9th	*Innergellie* to Aberdeen for	£2,500
Dec. 28th	*Largo Bay* to Aberdeen for	£3,100

1901

Feb. 22nd	*Fife Ness* to Aberdeen for	£3,200
Sep. 13th	*Rob the Ranter* to Anster for	£900

The Proclamation of Edward VIII by Provost Carstairs in Anster.
In the background the fishing fleet wait, with steam up, to depart for the
winter herring

The crew of the Cellardyke steam drifter *Unity*. Skipper David Corstorphine is on the extreme left, with son William crouching front left. Other crew members pictured include A. Stevenson, J. Stevenson, C. Marr and P. Murray.

The Cellardyke steam drifter *Olive Leaf* berthed in Anster harbour

Nov. 29th	*Newark Castle* to Shields for	£1,650
Dec. 8th	*Maggie Lauder* to Shields for	£850
	(Later sunk in Loch Fyne, 1903)	
Dec. 27th	*Isle of May* to Saltcoats for	£1,650

1902

Jan. 10th	*Kellie Castle* to London for	£1,950
Jan. 24th	*County of Fife* to W.of Scot	£1,850
Sep. 12th	*William Tennant* to D.Wood, Cellardyke	
Sep. 12th	*Anster Fair* to T.Anderson, Pittenweem	

1903

Feb.27th	*Rothesay Bay* to Aberdeen	£2,300

1905

Jan. 27th	*Innergellie* to J.Muir, Cellardyke.

In June 1900, it was mentioned that there was a boom in boat building which meant, specifically, sailing boats with steam capstans. Fulton of Pittenweem had orders for eight. Two of them, *Cornucopia* for T. Bett of Cellardyke and *Pride o' Fife* for John Watson, Cellardyke, were launched in December.

1901

In January, the number of children on the school roll in Cellardyke was 556. Today, May 1997, this number has dropped to 240. Compare the Census returns for 1891 and 1901 with today's population, which only exceeded 3,000 in 1981 for the United Burghs of Anster and Cellardyke. In 1901 the population was closer to 5,000

	1901	1891
Anster Easter	1187	1134
Anster Wester	558	593
Kilrenny and Cellardyke	2934	2998
Pittenweem	1007	1991
St. Monans	2005	1998
Crail	1531	1613

51

5th July: Stephen Williamson retired from business, so the influence of the real originator of the local steam liners had gone. He was born in Cellardyke in 1827 and, amongst many other charitable donations he made to his birthplace, he built Chalmers Church and Waid Tower. His retirement was not a long one for he died on June 19th 1903.

6th September: Opening of Anster Easter school, which became part of the Waid Academy in 1924.

1902

24th. October: A. Thomson, boat builder, completed a yawl for Crail. It was his 26th yawl and he had built most of them for Crail. We had two of them and I didn't like them. My father said some of them were built in what is now the yard of the Fisheries Museum.

At Yarmouth the sailing boat *Vanguard*, KY603, had 130 crans. She was owned by Martin Gardner and his sons who were Henry, John, Martin, and Tom. Of these sons, Martin was said to be the greatest fisher of his day. Old Martin by this time had probably become the harbour master.

Steam drifters tightly packed into the Inner Harbour at Anster

The Pittenweem steam drifter KY149 *Restless Wave*

The steam drifter *Vanguard III* in Anster. She was built at South Shields for the Gardner family and was the first steel steam drifter to be built for the East Fife Fishing Fleet

The Steam Drifter and the Demise of Sail

1903

11th December: *Vanguard III*, KY 693, launched at South Shields
for M. Gardner and Sons. Her deck was 82' long by 11'3" wide
and she had a depth of 9'. She was built of steel and was the first of
her kind for East Fife. I can't find out much more about her, although I have turned over many pages in the *East Fife Record*.
Perhaps I missed something, but I was surprised to find so little
about her, as she was the progenitor of the real steam drifter (S.D.)
fleet in the East Neuk of Fife. The Gardner family were to have
another two drifters built, and I can remember seeing one of them.
There are still descendants of that Martin Gardner living in Anster
who are still engaged in the fishing.

1906

2nd March: Miller launched a new sailing boat for James Mackay
of St.Monans, named *Marjory*. Her dimensions were 70' by 22' by
9'.

This is the last sail boat built for a local owner which I've been
able to trace, although there were some built for other places. Up
to this time, only sailing vessels had pursued the winter herring
fishing, but in a northerly wind the steam drifter *Vanguard* shot a
fleet of nets in Dunbar Bay, where the sailing boats were afraid to
go near the shore. It landed a shot of 33 crans, gaining £100 for
the shot.

11th May: Fulton built the first steam drifter for an East Fife
owner, George Horsburgh, whose family had a sailing boat *Preston
Horsburgh*. The owner's daughter Liza Horsburgh christened the
new boat *Preston*, KY 121. She measured 90' overall, with a beam

of 19'. She was equipped with first class compound engines at Leith.

10th August: Steam drifter *St Ayles*, KY122, launched by Miller at Anstruther for J. Stewart, Cellardyke. She had an 84' keel and was 18'6" wide by 8'6".

My friend the late James Brunton said she was the smallest of the local steam drifters and was quite speedy. She had six berths in the fore cabin and four in the aft cabin, the first evidence I've found of a drifter having a crew of 10. The steam liners only carried a crew of 9. The tenth person would be required to coil the messenger rope, and was also required to be the cook.

All the local boat builders were now building steam drifters and there were said to be 16 or 17 orders from local skippers. Another drifter was launched by Miller for the Gardner Brothers; Alex, John and Philip of Cellardyke. Christened the *Maggies*, she measured 85' by 18'6" by 8'6". Her registration was KY138.

1907

January 18th: Miller launched a steam drifter in Anster near to where the British Legion hut used to be, on the north side of the Outer Harbour. She was built for A. Aitken and Sons, St Monans and christened the *Camellia*, KY 149. She was 85' by 18'6".

For the next couple of years, the demand was so great for wooden steam drifters that several of the local boats were built at Portgordon. This included the *Morning Star*, KY 128, built for D. Watson and others. He was known as Star Davie, who had a brother Star Alex and a son Star Jeems. At the time of the launching of their drifter, they still owned a sailing boat *Morning Star*, KY190, owned by D.& J. Watson. Lest you should think this was accidental let me quote from a missive I received from my friend Harry Watson, author of the book *"Kilrenny and Cellardyke"*:

56

The steam drifter *Morning Star* in Anster harbour

Steam drifter KY122 *St Ayles* entering Great Yarmouth. She was the last drifter to land over 100 cran of herring in Anster.

Steam drifter KY220 *Olive Leaf* in Pittenweem harbour

Register Book, Anstruther, 1824-26

No.17/1826, 30th June 1824.

Morning Star

Burthen: Twenty 76/94 Tons.

Built: This present year at Leith, by William Lindsay.

Master: Alexander Watson, Junior.

Decks: None.

Masts: Two, length 35ft 7ins.

Breadth: Above the main wales - 12ft, 2 3/4 ins.

Depth: 4ft. 9 ins.

Lugger-rigged, with a running bowsprit, round sterned, clench built. Sole owner (64 shares) Alexander Watson of the town of Cellardyke and Parish of Kilrenny in the County of Fife.

(Sold on 31st October, 1844).

N.B. This *Morning Star* of 1824 had a round stern, so she was obviously not a 'Fifie'.
Alas, there is no Star Alex, or Star Davie or Star Jeems, descendants of the first Star Alex, at the fishing today. There are, however, two of his descendants painting seascapes as artists; James Watson in Anster and Allan Watson, now living in Cupar. The story does not end there. The last Star Jeems, who owned the steam drifter

Morning Star, sold the drifter immediately after the First World War to the Rodger family, great nephews of Cpt. Rodger of China Clipper fame. The Rodger family had lost their steam drifter *Craignoon* during the war and when they purchased the *Morning Star* they refused to change the name. The authorities wouldn't allow two Steam Drifters named *Morning Star* under KY registration, so when the last Star Jeems bought one of the steel standard drifters after the war, he named her *Stella Aurora*.

With steam drifters built all over the country for local owners in this pre-war period, I thought I would look for the last one built locally for local owners. I never found anything later than March 6th 1908, when the steam drifter *Lizzie Hutt*, measuring 86' by 21' by 10', was launched by Miller at Anster for J. Hutt and Chapman Innes of St. Monans.

Some people will still recall her as a wreck bought by Jock Buchan, farmer at Caiplie, to the east of Cellardyke. She lay on the shore at Caiplie for many years, while Jock Buchan extracted all the scrap metal from her. Several years ago, some youths set the remaining wood on fire and, in the summer of 1990, only the rudder could be seen down among the rocks. This is one of the few remaining relics of the age of steam drifters.

Quite a few steel drifters were built for local owners right up to the start of the First World War, including the *Plough* and *Kilmany* for M. Gardner Senior and Sons, *Lily and Maggie* for A. P. & J. Gardner, and *Carmi III* for T. Anderson.

To give an idea of the advance of the steam drifter and the eclipse of the sailing boat, on the following pages I will give the full list of the East Neuk steam drifter fleet in 1914. Notice that the names will include those steam liners that were converted to steam drifters.

The St Monans steam drifter ML122 *Lizzie Hutt*

The Cellardyke drifter *Twinkling Star* KY347, whose skipper Jim Muir was regarded as the greatest local skipper between the wars. She was originally owned by the father of north-east fisherman poet Peter Buchan

Davie Wood on board Star Jeems' drifter *Stella Aurora*. He was owner of the Steam Liner *William Tennant* from 1902 until the First World War. Davie's daughter married Star Jeems' son

Steam drifter KY300 *Carmi III* in Anster harbour

1914: Steam Drifters of the East Neuk Fishing Ports

	Boat	Owners
St Monans		
ML122	*Lizzie Hutt*	Jas Hutt, C.Innes, EIiza.Hutt
MLI23	*Christina Mayes*	John Mayes.
MLI25	*Mackays*	R., T. & Jas Mackay
ML126	*Janet Reekie*	W.R.D.A. & C. Reekie.
KY143	*Camellia*	A.Aitken, P. & R. Aitken
KY152	*Pursuit*	H. Bett.
ML164	*Diligence*	T. & A. Adam.
ML172	*Bruces*	R.V. & J. Mackay. P.Marr.
Pittenwecm		
KY121	*Preston*	G. Horsburgh.
KY134	*Andrina*	W. & A. Anderson.
KY149	*Restless Wave*	R. Hughes Sen.
KY169	*Azarael*	W. Lawson.
KY188	*Maggie Leask*	W. Black.
KY201	*Tulip*	M. Hughes.
KY217	*Magdalen*	J. Hughes Montador.
KY267	*Calceolaria*	W. Hutchison.
KY461	*Anster Fair*	T. Anderson.
Anster and Cellardyke		
KY8	*Lily and Maggie*	J. Gardner.
KY71	*Dreel Castle*	I. & W. Sutherland.
KY73	*Cromorna*	A. Henderson.
KY94	*White Queen*	J. Birrell.
KY97	*Rothesay Bay*	J. Stewart.
KY103	*St. Adrian*	J. Hodge.
KY105	*Daisy*	R. Watson.
KY107	*Golden Strand*	J. Stevenson.
KY109	*Eva*	J. Birrell.
KY116	*Coreopsis*	P. Gardner.

Anster and Cellardyke (Cont.)

KY120	*Alnwick Castle*	A. Lothian.
KY122	*St. Ayles*	J. Stewart.
KY127	*Vine*	A. Parker.
KY128	*Morning Star*	D. Watson.
KY138	*Maggies*	P. Gardner.
KY139	*Scot*	H. Bell.
KY140	*Plough*	M. Gardner.
KY160	*Camperdown*	J. Muir.
KY162	*Unity*	D. Corstorphine.
KY163	*Primrose*	R. Melville.
KY176	*East Neuk*	Jas. Smith.
KY178	*Integrity*	G. Anderson.
KY179	*White Rose*	Jas. Muir.
KY189	*Evening Star*	R. Hughes.
KY199	*Venus*	W. Smith.
KY210	*Alices*	H. Bett.
KY218	*Pride o' Fife*	J. Watson.
KY220	*Olive Leaf*	W. Smith.
KY251	*Violet*	W. Watson.
KY253	*Breadwinner*	H. Bett.
KY276	*Hiedra*	J. Smith.
KY279	*Craignoon*	A. Rodger.
KY283	*Guerdon*	A. Reid & W. S. Bonthron
KY300	*Carmi III*	T. Anderson.
KY304	*Kilmany*	M. Gardner.
KY459	*Rob the Ranter*	J. Brunton.
KY460	*Edith*	P. Brown & A. Watson.
KY472	*William Tennant*	D. Wood.
KY493	*Glenogil*	R. Stewart.
KY571	*White Cross*	A. Gourlay.
KY604	*Innergellie*	J. Muir (Keay).
KY693	*Vanguard III*	M. Gardner.

The *Breadwinner* KY253 departing from Anster harbour. She was launched in Anster in 1907 for Henry Bett and his sons Tom and Henry. Tom's son, young Henry, became her skipper at a very young age before the Second World War owing to his father's illness and is today the only surviving pre-war skipper of a steam drifter

Steam drifter KY162 *Unity*. She was built in 1907 in St Monans for David Corstorphine of Cellardyke

Steam drifter KY152 *Pursuit*

There was a total of 59 steam drifters in the East Neuk before the First World War.

The last article on Scottish fisheries that I could find pre-war was in the *East Fife Record*, June 4th 1914, which said that 1913 was a record year for Scottish fisheries.

Local fishery statistics were as follows:

	1912	1913
Sailing Boats	421	373
Creels	4290	4340
Motor Boats	10	27
Steam Drifters	60	64 (Highest)
Fishermen (local)	1385	1386
Non resident	552	368
Coopers	104	

To complete the pre- First World War era, an excellent article on the first experiments in applying steam to the fishing industry is given by James Ritchie of the Fishing News. It is too long to copy here, but two points may be mentioned:

"Its success and development since 1899 is well known. At that time, the bush rope now in use had not been introduced. It was after its adoption that the rapid advance in the size and construction of the herring boat took place. Fishing in rough weather then became a possibility"

"Fraserburgh's first move for steam was in 1892 when its steam liner Philworth *was built. In the following year the* Pioneer *was built by a Peterhead company for steam lining. Peterhead however, now leads with steam drifters"*.

The Post War Years

1920 is the first post-war almanac I've been able to see and it does not contain any of the 'Standard Drifters' which had been built during the First World War. Standard Drifters were to prove the backbone of the drifter fleet between the wars. Surprising it was to see that the total for the East Neuk ports was 59 steam drifters.

Standard Drifters still did not appear in 1922, although the total number of steam drifters had gone down to 53. I haven't seen the almanacs for 1923, 1924 or 1925, but by 1926 the Standard Drifters had appeared and the total number of steam drifters in the local fleet was just short of 60. As it was never again to touch this figure, I will give the names and owners of the East Neuk boats for this year:

	Boat	Owners
St Monans		
ML69	Pansy	Jas. and John Allan.
ML119	Lena & Francis	M. Hughes.
ML122	Lizzie Hutt	J. Hutt and C. Innes.
KY4	Pride of Buchan	W. & J. Wood.
KY32	Faithlie	T. Gowans.
KY98	Mare Vivemus	J. Anderson & W.S. Bonthron.
KY138	Maggies	J. Reekie, W. Fortune, J.Graham.
KY143	Camellia	P. & R. Aitken.
KY148	Eventide	D. Smith.
KY172	Lucy Mackay	W. Mackay, W. Meldrum.
KY208	Ocean Angler	R. Marr.
KY214	Honey Bee	R.D.C.& A. Reekie.
KY571	White Cross	J. Graham, D. Smith.

The steam drifter *Ocean Angler* berthed at the end of the East Pier at St Monans

The steam drifter *Acorn* was skippered by one of the many East Neuk fishermen named Martin Gardner. 'Acorn Mairt', as he was known locally, was also coxwain of the Anstruther Lifeboat and it was his seamanship that saved the lifeboat on the same night the Arbroath Lifeboat was lost

The Pittenweem steam drifter *Restless Wave*

The steam drifter *Copious*

Boat		Owners
Pittenweem		
KY26	*Silver Scale*	Jessie Watson.
KY34	*Retriever*	J. & R. Wood.
KY121	*Preston*	G. Horsburgh.
KY149	*Restless Wave*	R. G. & J. Hughes.
KY169	*Azarael*	W. Lawson.
KY188	*Golden Sunray*	W. Black.
KY220	*Olive Leaf*	D. Black.

Anster and Cellardyke		
KY52	*Anster Belle*	J. Graham & W. Birrell.
KY73	*Cromorna*	R.Gardner,G. Doig,W.S.Bonthron.
KY94	*White Queen*	A. Birrell & R. Moncrieff.
KY134	*Scot*	H. Bett
KY45	*Stella Aurora*	D. & J. Watson.
KY175	*Copious*	A.J&P.Gardner,J.Graham, N.Wilson.
KY18	*Agnes Gardner*	J.Gardner, G&T.Melville, W. Wilson.
KY14	*Cassiopeia*	J.B.& W.Wilson, D.Watson, W.C.Wilson.
KY16	*Refloresco*	J. & A. Muir.
KY19	*Spes Melior*	W. Moncrieff & others.
KY20	*Bene Vertat*	A. Reid & I. Barclay.
KY21	*Cosmea*	W.C.Wilson, J. Boyter, D. Christie.
KY23	*Kincraig*	T. Birrell & others.
KY25	*Lasher*	J. Brunton, C. Barclay.
KY27	*Fife Ness*	E. Irvin.
KY33	*Thorntree*	W. Wood.
KY48	*Pilot Star*	D. Smith. P.Gardner. W.W.Carstairs.
KY62	*Uberous*	T. D.& R. Boyter, J. Stevenson.
KY95	*Abdeil*	L.Robertson, W.S.Bonthron, L.Horsburgh
KY97	*Rothesay Bay*	J. Stewart, R. & W. Murray.
KY71	*Dreel Castle*	T. Cunningham & others.
KY300	*Carmi III*	T. Anderson.

Boat		Owners
Anster and Cellardyke (Cont.)		
KY495	*Glenogil*	T. Cunningham & others.
KY105	*Daisy*	A.Reid, D.Christie.
KY122	*St. Ayles*	J. Stewart.
KY128	*Morning Star*	A.Rodger & others.
KY162	*Unity*	D. Corstorphine & others.
KY163	*Primrose*	G. & T. Melville.
KY178	*Integrity*	R. Copeland.
KY189	*Evening Star*	R. Hughes.
KY194	*Acorn*	W. Wilson, M. Gardner.
KY199	*Venus*	W. Smith.
KY210	*Alices*	H. W. & J. Bett.
KY218	*Pride o' Fife*	J. Watson & others.
KY224	*Mace*	M. Gardner Sen. & Jun.
KY228	*Norman Wilson*	J. Gardner, W.C. Wilson.
KY232	*Menat*	M. & R. Gardner.
KY251	*Violet*	W. Watson & others.
KY253	*Breadwinner*	H. & T. Bett.

Standard Drifters

Many of these boats were Standard Drifters with a North Shields shareholder, W.C. Wilson.

The Standard Drifter had an 86'6" keel, an 18'6" to 19' beam and overall measured 92'6".

Pittenweem and St. Monans had no Standard boats at this time.

The *Refloresco* was specially built in 1926 for the Muir family. The *William Wilson*, KY 293, was built for W. C. Wilson of North

Standard Drifters berthed in the Inner Harbour at Anster during the 1930's

The steam drifter *Wilson Line*. She was the largest and also the last of the steam drifters

Shields and was skippered by J. Wilson of Cellardyke.
The *Wilson Line*, KY 322, was also built for W. C. Wilson of
North Shields. Her skipper was D.Watson of Cellardyke. The
collection of dues in Anster said she was 101 ft overall, the largest
and last steam drifter built in Scotland. This did not balance the
wastage as wooden drifters gradually disappeared, being unable to
go as far to sea as the Standard Drifters, which were magnificent
sea boats.

The Distribution of Steam Drifters in the East of Fife

Year	St.Monans	Pittenweem	Anster & Cellardyke
1928	10	5	36
1930	10	6	35
1932	10	4	32
1934	10	4	33
1936	7	3	30
1939	5	0	19

Many of the older wooden drifters were scrapped and Pittenweem
had none after 1936. Does that give part of the reason for the fish
market being at Pittenweem today?

As happened with the liners in the First World War, when the
Government conscripted them for active service as minesweepers,
the steam drifters, too, were quickly called up for naval service in
1939. After the war only three came back; *Cosmea*, later to be
named *Coriedalis*, the *William Wilson* and the *Wilson Line*. All
three were partly owned by W.C. Wilson of Shields for a few years
then sold in 1954. Several other drifters came to the East Neuk on
loan and John Muir bought the *Sea Reaper* in 1954.
It is fitting to close with John Muir and his brother Jim Muir, as the

story of steam fishing in East Fife started with the steam liners. John was the last fisherman to go to the gartlins as skipper of an East Fife boat in his motor boat *Ocean Dawn*, KY371. John retired in April 1984. His brother Jim was generally regarded locally as the greatest fisherman of his day. He was the winner of the Prunier Trophy in 1957 at Great Yarmouth in the M.B. *Silver Chord*, KY 124, for having the highest catch at Yarmouth or Lowestoft that year. In the previous year, 1956, he skippered the *Coriedalis,* the last steam drifter to go to the Yarmouth fishing from Scotland.

The steam drifter *Cosmea*, later named the *Coriedalis*. As the *Coriedalis*, she was the last Scottish steam drifter to fish at Great Yarmouth in 1956

The *Spes Aurea*, KY81, taking a big sea at Yarmouth

Appendix I

The Fishing Grounds

When I asked George Muir, middle brother of the three fisherman sons of John Muir of the *Spes Aurea*, to make a sound tape for the Scottish Fisheries Museum, he included the names of the areas where the Dykers were wont to shoot their gartlins in the North Sea. Some of these places are on the charts and some of them are known only to the East Fife fishermen.

With George and Jim both dead, and it should not be forgotten that Jim was the greatest of the East Fife fishermen of his day, I called on John, the youngest of the Muir brothers to ask him to mark the areas mentioned by his late brother George. This he did, so I will name them with the warning that some are not mentioned on charts but known only to the Dykers, e.g. 'Arthur of Arthur's Hard' was the nickname of one of the many Martin Gardner skippers.

What follows on the next page is the list obtained from John Muir, the last skipper to go to the gartlins as pursued by the East Fife fishermen. He also gave the latitude and longitude when marking the chart but these I have not included here as there are still East Fife fishermen pursuing the seine net and pair trawling today, and to some this knowledge may be an advantage whilst others may be disadvantaged.

John Muir's List of Grounds:

Viking
The Patch
Reef
58 Line
Edge of Deep
Tongue
Red Sands
Arthurs Hard
Half Moons
West Bank
Sutherland's Rough
Jubilee Bank
Mandel Rough
Little Fisher

John Muir acknowledged that, latterly, he went with stronger tackle than his elders used and that, when fully shot, the great line stretched for fourteen miles, compared with the previous average of twelve miles.

As the Muir's finished up with a diesel engine motor boat, the larger fuel capacity enabled them to go further afield than the steam drifter was able to go. For instance, the motor boat could carry enough diesel to take them to Rockall and back, with fuel to spare, whereas the steam drifter could only risk that distance in clement summer weather with a good forecast, otherwise their coal would be used up before they got home.

The steam drifter *Evening Star*, built in 1907 for R.Hughes of Cellardyke

The Cellardyke drifter *Olive Leaf*, later sold to St. Monans where she was re-named *Casimir*. The author's uncle, Dave Smith, is standing third from the right between D.Dick and J.Murray. Among the other crew members on deck are J.Cunningham, J.Smith, D.Tawse, and W.Smith

Appendix II

Feeding the Crew

Before the Second World War, when John Muir went to sea with his brother Jim, a typical breakfast eaten on leaving port would be porridge, followed by ham and egg or sausage.
Whilst at sea, the porridge would be followed by fried Jumbo (large) Haddock.
Dinner and Tea would consist of boiled Cod or Ling. Occasionally the crew would be treated to Sea Cat, skinned and fried. This was regarded as a delicacy.

After the war, Halibut caught in deep water were often covered in sea lice, which would suck out the blood and make the fish unsaleable. These would be skinned and fried and served up to the crew.

The storage of bread was a great problem at sea up until the Second World War. Each day, the moulded part of the bread had to be cut away, causing much of the loaf to be wasted. After the war, a drifter crew observed a German trawler loading a bag net of loaves straight into the ice compartment. That solved the bread problem!

Alex Anderson, a fisherman who went with the steam drifters to Yarmouth, recalls that if the boat was in port during the week you got porridge and boiled egg for Breakfast. For Tea, kippers were served up if the boat was lucky enough to have acquired a free box.

A typical menu for a week's fishing at Yarmouth, as recalled by Alex Anderson, is given overleaf.

<u>Meals served on board a Steam Drifter whilst fishing at Yarmouth</u>

<u>Monday</u>
Breakfast: Porridge
Dinner: Mince and Potatoes
Tea: Salt Herring

<u>Tuesday</u>
Breakfast: Herring
Dinner: Soup or Kale
Tea: Cheese or Sausages

<u>Wednesday</u>
Breakfast: Herring
Dinner: 3lb Roast

<u>Thursday</u>
Breakfast: Herring
Dinner: Stew

<u>Friday</u>
Breakfast: Herring
Dinner: Kale or Soup

<u>Saturday</u>
Breakfast: Herring
Dinner: Steak and Onions
Tea: Cheese and Tomatoes

<u>Sunday</u>
Breakfast: Bacon and Egg
Dinner: 4lb Roast with Cabbage or Cauliflower
followed by Apple Tart or Duff
Tea: Cheese and Tomatoes

On days where only Breakfast and Dinner are listed, Tea would consist of
Bread with Jam, Syrup or Treacle. Sweets during the week were Rice,
Creamola or Semolina.

Hauling the Gartlins on board the *Pride o' Fife* using a steam operated line hauler

The herring fleet wait to enter Anster harbour during the
1930's

In Summary

We started with the steam liners in the 1890s. The shortcoming of these boats was that their usefulness extended only to the end of the summer months when most of the fishermen went south to catch the herrings which appeared in large shoals off the Yarmouth and Lowestoft coasts. The steam liners were unfortunately inclined to tear the nets and, for this reason, were superseded by the steam drifters which were slightly smaller but more manoeuvrable

The first of the steam drifters was the steel built *Vanguard III*, launched by Smiths Dock at Shields. By 1908, greet fleets of wooden steam drifters were built all round the north-east Fife coast. Firstly the *Preston* for Pittenweem, then the *St. Ayles* for Cellardyke and the *Camellia* for St Monans. Many lasted into the 1930s, with the *Cosmea (Coriedalis)* being the last Scottish steam drifter to go to the Yarmouth fishing.

The Standard Drifters, built during the First World War, proved to be the best all round fishing vessel in the age of steam. It is interesting to consider a Standard Steam Drifter's annual life cycle. After the First World War, the local winter herring was pursued for the first three months of the year, mainly by 'bauldies', motor boats, or a few of the wooden drifters. The Standard Drifters, meanwhile, went to the West Coast or the Shetland area and worked the great lines, if they caught enough herrings for bait. But, as the winter herring approached its climax In 1935 and 1936, all of the Standard Drifters except the *Agnes Gardner* took part in the winter herring. The latter drifter pursued the great lines throughout the year except for the period of the herring fishing at Yarmouth.

April, May and part of June occupied all of the steam drifters at the great lines, the larger Standard Drifters always venturing further afield. Robbie Gardner's grandfather, William Smith, fished from Hartlepool in the *Venus*, a wooden pre-1914 steam drifter. The *Venus* landed every week, while the larger Standard Drifters would take ten to fourteen days to accomplish one trip, landing mainly in North Shields.

These Standard Drifters were mainly steel built although seven or eight in the East Fife area were made of wood. The *Uberous* is an example and, from the photograph of her included, it can be seen that they were distinguished by having their stern rail turned in. These wooden drifters had planks of one and a half to one and three quarter inches thick. The steel Standard Drifters were constructed from 5/16" steel plates.

By June the majority of the Standard Drifters would give up lines and go to the Summer Herring Drave. As our Lammas Drave had ceased before the First World War, they would start about Wick and work their way south, finishing up by mid September on the Northumberland coast, when a few shots would be landed in Anstruther on Friday or Saturday to give the crews a weekend at home.

By mid September they would all come home, including those that remained working the great lines instead of going to the Drave. All would then prepare for Yarmouth, from where they would fish for the herring for 8-10 weeks, during which time each member of the crew would salt down for themselves a quarter of a barrel of herring so that nobody need go hungry in the district as there would always be a dish of 'tatties and herring' to fall back on.

And so the year's cycle was complete.

The steam drifter KY62 *Uberous*, owned by the Boyter family

Another view of *Uberous* in Anster harbour. She was a wooden Standard
Drifter and, as can be seen in this photograph, had her stern rail turned in

Index

92

93

Star Alex 56, 59
Star Davie 56, 59
Star Jeems 56, 59, 62
Steam Capstan
	7, 18, 28, 31, 43, 44, 47, 51
Steam Drifters 55, 63, 87
Steam Liners 8, 16, 24, 28, 87
Steam Trawlers 8, 11, 12
Stella Aurora 60, 62, 71
Stirling 7
Strike 39
Summer Herring Drave 15, 88
Sutherland W.   14

T

Taes 12, 15
Tawse A. 15
Teal Duck 24
Telephone Service 36
Thorntree 71
Toiler 11
Trawl Fishing 16
Tulip 17, 63
Twinkling Star 61

U

Uberous 71, 88, 89
Unity 6, 50, 37, 64, 72

V

Vanguard 40, 52
Vanguard III 54, 55, 64, 87
Venus 64, 72, 88
Vine 64
Violet 64, 72

W

Waid Academy 52
Waid Tower 11, 52

Watson David (Pip) 15, 23
Watson Salter 4
West Coast 87
White Cross
	35, 40, 41, 48, 64, 68
White Cross Fishing Co. 32
White Queen 63, 71
White Rose 64
White Star Fishing Co. 32
Wick 88
William Beat 7
William Tennant 24, 25, 51, 62, 64
William Wilson 72, 75
Williamson Stephen 8, 12, 16,
	27, 28, 44, 52
Wilson W. C. 72, 75
Wilson Line 74, 75
Winter Herring Fishing 15, 87
Wood Davie 62

Y

Yarmouth
	15, 48, 76, 78, 84, 87, 88

List of Illustrations

Illustrations (Continued)